INTERFERON, OR ON THEATER

FIELD TRANSLATION SERIES 7

Miroslav Holub

INTERFERON, OR ON THEATER

Translated by Dana Hábová
and David Young

Introduction by David Young

FIELD Translation Series 7

Grateful acknowledgement is made to the following magazines in which some of these translations originally appeared: *FIELD, Discover, Malahat Review*

Publication of this book was made possible through a grant from the Ohio Arts Council.

Library of Congress Cataloging in Publication Data
    Holub, Miroslav (translated by Dana Hábová and
    David Young)
        INTERFERON, or ON THEATER
            (The FIELD Translation Series; v. 7)

LC: 82-082128

ISBN: 0-932440-12-6
        0-932440-13-4 (paperback)

CONTENTS

The Merry Adventures of the Puppets

Endgames

INTRODUCTION
by David Young

It is a pleasure and a privilege to introduce
Miroslav Holub's new collection to English-
speaking readers. This major figure in postwar
European poetry has, to my mind, here ex-
ceeded his remarkable previous accomplish-
ments. *Interferon, or On Theater* is mostly the re-
sult of four productive years, 1979 to 1982, and is
impressive both in its freshness — some of the
poems were written and translated within a
week or two of the manuscript's completion in
May of 1982 — and in its unity: for all its great
range of materials and forms, it has a tightness
and interconnectedness that few collections of
poetry achieve. This unity is both a reflection of
earlier tendencies in Holub's work and a culmi-
nation of them. He has always been conscious of
the advantages of careful design, but he has
never carried them out in such an extensive and
effective fashion.

The double title furnishes one clue to the way
the book works, by identifying its two major
metaphors, one from the world of immunologi-
cal research that constitutes Holub's other pro-
fession, and one from the history of human at-

tempts to understand the world by artificial and imaginative representations of it. While the book seems to move from the biological metaphor to the theatrical one, from a first section called "Biological Poems" through middle sections titled "Towards a Theory of the Theater" and "The Merry Adventures of the Puppets," to the theater pieces called "Endgames" that close the collection, both metaphors in fact function throughout, like the parallel rails of a track. Poems in the first section include both glancing ("Biodrama") and extended ("Interferon") considerations of the theatrical, while "stage poems" in the last section like "The Angel of Death" continue to draw substantially on the knowledge and insights Holub derives from laboratory science. The long and moving poem "Interferon," the effective center of this collection, shows us how this is possible by revealing that the two metaphors are really one. Interference on the cellular level corresponds to the presence of theater in our lives; both are attempts to arrest and mesmerize destructive forces, disease and history, attempts that may succeed in the short run and fail in the long. The body goes from life to eventual death, but along the way it fights some successful and stirring battles in its own defense. History may operate similarly; we cannot ward off its deprivations and holocausts, but our resistance, our imaginative response, has a meaning and merit of its own. Moreover, our consciousness of how these things work — whether it comes from gazing through a microscope or sensing the presence of roles and performances in our lives (as when the bystanders in "Collision" form a ring to become audience for the most elementary kind of theater, watching a death) — gives us a richer understanding and a means for confronting and enduring events that might otherwise shatter us.

II

This book, then, includes harsh truths about life and history, and in doing so it reflects its roots in the literature and experience of postwar Europe. What the populations of countries like Poland, Czechoslovakia, Hungary and Yugoslavia (not to mention those of Germany and Russia, of France, Italy, Spain and England) endured, has inevitably shaped their literature by forcing it to a crisis of identity and function: in a world of war, of holocaust, of political oppression, what value does language have? What sense can literature make? How can art apply to, let alone enhance, life? Finding answers to these difficult questions has produced a literature that is often outer-directed, with an attachment to objects and an impersonal manner. A preference has developed for what Holub has described to me as "the fully exposed poem," one whose structure and manner are so direct that weak or naive content simply can't survive in it. Reduction is another leading principle of this literature, the result of a sort of basic survival training: "When you can't say everything, you say next to nothing," as Holub puts it. The impersonality is also often a necessary form of camouflage: "You leave yourself out of the poem because you can't put yourself in."

These characteristics define Holub's immediate literary heritage, additionally colored in the case of Czech literature by a strong current of folklore and a dour wit. What this new book shows is how Holub has gradually modified that heritage for his own purposes. He does not, for example, exclude himself as rigorously as he has in the past. These poems often allow personal recollection and individual reflection a greater role than heretofore in Holub. Some of the poems are clearly occasional. "Interferon" was initiated in part by the death of Holub's great contemporary, the poet Vladimir Holan. "Collision" commemorates the death of a man who was Holub's friend and teacher. "Landscapes" and "United Flight 412" are love poems. "Sunday" contains a vivid memory of trains headed for the death camps in World War II. And "Memo for a Little Daughter," "Half a Hedgehog," and the closing stanzas of "Seeing" all rise vividly from personal family experiences. That Holub now mixes these personal elements into his fundamentally impersonal style testifies both to his artistic growth and confidence, and to his response to other poetic traditions, such as the American contemporary one. The result is a poetry that increases its power through the broader range of possibilities it commands.

III

The fact that Holub is a noted research scientist has been much remarked. Substantial achievement in two different fields is very rare, and a writer who can bridge the two cultures is rightly prized.* But it remains to ask just how the science informs the poetry, what it means in practice. I would emphasize the wider horizons

---

*See, for example, Bruce Schechter, "Miroslav Holub: A Man for Two Cultures," in *Discover* (May, 1982), pp. 60-64.

it makes possible for the poem. There is simply more knowledge to bring to bear on a given subject at a given moment. The middle section of "Collision," a litany of suffering and pain, includes memories of a dying girl in a leukemia ward and an orangutan seen in a zoo, but it also contains "the first genes / accumulating amino acids" as life began, an expansion of the poem's time-frame, and the birth of stars from "giant molecular cloud complexes," a similar expansion of its space-frame. Just as in the poetry of John Donne and other metaphysicals of the 17th century, the surprising range of reference enlarges our sense of what sorts of things can be compared, breaking down barriers between different forms of knowledge and asserting a unity in the world, an affinity between microcosm and macrocosm.

The scientific vantage point is also useful for achieving the kind of distance and perspective I have said Holub requires to come to terms with the world he lives in. As personal emotion and recollection come to play a larger part in his work, this means of achieving detachment becomes even more vital to him. It can produce a thoughtful irony, as with Immanuel Kant, in the poem of that title, ignorant in his hypochondria of how his own immunological processes, "The starry sky of non-self, / perfectly mirrored / deep inside," make him a walking critique of pure reason. It can expand the context of suffering so as to help make it bearable, as in "Half a Hedgehog," where another litany rises to a strange climax of "double helices, purines / and pyrimidines." And it affords the kind of dark comedy that characterizes poems like "Teaching about Arthropods."

Finally, on the subject of poetry's strengthening by science, I should say that scientific method has shown Holub that metaphor can be used as hypothesis, an instrument for testing experience through conjecture and experiment. Perhaps that is true for every poet, but it may well be that the process of experimentation in the lab has sharpened Holub's sense of freedom to let comparison function as supposition and provisional theory. I will cite two passages in support of this idea. The first is from "Memo for a Little Daughter":

When we're away, the home we leave behind
shrinks to a little oval mirror
and our parents act
in the theater of flies

that we know nothing about
because it's a play
beneath the play
and soon night falls.

This is about the solipsism or mild paranoia that makes us suspect that the world ceases to exist when we are not present to observe it. By this point in the poem concessions to the continuation of that existence are being made, and they come here in the form of shrunken scale — our home and our parents may exist, but they become insignificant in size and hence in meaning — as projected through the free-floating metaphor of theater that pervades the book. In a theater existence is both false — merely a performance, a show — and true — a heightening of the ordinary. The experiments in comparison serve to test the validity of the familiar emotion: they are a kind of critique of it, acknowledging its power but questioning its validity.

My second example is from "Collision":

The streetcar stood jammed over him
like an icebreaker's bow; what was left
of the car was a funny pretzel
bitten by the dentures of a mad angel.

Something dark was dripping onto the rails,
and a surprisingly pale wind
leafed through the pages of a book
that was still warm.

The multiplicity of the comparisons in the first sentence — icebreaker, pretzel, angel's dentures — suggests an experimental attitude; in the attempt to do justice to the strangeness of the moment, the poet does not feel constrained by consistency or decorum. The swerve into reticence — "something dark" — and personification — the book-browsing wind — in the second sentence also illustrates how readily the style and manner can shift to accommodate changes in subject and tone. The agility and brilliance of this passage may not be exclusively those of a scientist (consider how few scientists can write and think that way!), but they may owe something to the poet's scientific training and experimental habits of mind.

IV

As my discussion has already implied, there are two distinct levels or uses of metaphor in this collection: the incidental comparisons of the kind found in the passage above, and the over-

arching metaphors of immunological process
and theater, mentioned earlier. These larger
metaphors are always ready to hand, as the pas-
sage about the "theater of flies" and "a play /
beneath the play" demonstrates. One can say
further that the book as a whole may be taken as
a giant experiment in seeing just how far the
metaphor of theater as life and as poetry can be
pushed. The book moves from sections that
make incidental but increasing use of theatrical
images and metaphors, to a section dominated
by one particular kind of theater, "The Merry
Adventures of the Puppets," a dark and sardonic
reading of history and social experiment that
culminates in the hilarious and agonizing per-
formance of the Sanskrit epic "Gilgamesh," as
presented by the puppet troupe (readers are
free to make whatever comparisons with recent
history they wish). It closes with a section of
theater pieces or "stage poems" in which poetry
actually *turns into* theater in form and manner,
disappearing into its own metaphor, so that po-
etry that is "on theater" is more fully realized
by experiment than we thought possible. Again,
I know of no other collection of poetry that
handles metaphor and its possibilities as an or-
ganizing and exploratory device so fully and

successfully. Holub's reach and daring are simply amazing.

V

The Miró painting on the cover of this book, selected by Holub himself, affords another useful perspective on the poet's work. Holub feels what he calls "a structural affinity" with Miró, whose work poses fundamental questions about art — how do you represent a sun, a star, a woman — that find their counterparts in Holub's handling of such diverse subjects as puppets, diseases, statues and teeth. One can imagine the theater pieces enacted against Miró backdrops, or the puppet epic printed with Miró illustrations. There is, in both these artists, along with the wild invention and playful fantasy, a somber and detached consideration of the human imagination, from its beginnings in history and in the experiences of children to its modern configurations and battles. The attitude toward imagination is simultaneously mocking and celebratory, tender and harsh. Both these artists help us feel a bit prouder of our peculiar and lamentable century. Without idealizing, they show us at our best.

VI

The translation of this book has benefitted enormously from Miroslav Holub's two residencies at Oberlin: in the spring semester of 1979, as playwright-in-residence, and in the spring semester of 1982, as Fulbright writer-in-residence. In the first of these visits the "Endgames," plays described as "stage poems" and constituting not entire dramas but only their conclusions, were first translated and some of them performed. During the second visit, the manuscript of *Interferon, or On Theater* was brought to completion — many of the poems were written in the four-month period of Holub's stay — and its entire translation was overseen by the poet. While FIELD's Translation Series would normally feature a different writer each time, our enthusiasm for this poet and this new collection, coupled with the opportunity to bring an exciting collection into print with unusual rapidity, overrode custom and made us decide to do a book by Holub for the second time in our brief history (the first, *Sagittal Section*, translated by Stuart Friebert and Dana Hábová, was published in 1980, number three in the series).

Most of the poems in this book were first translated by Dana Hábová, who works with Holub in Prague. Subsequently, all of them were brought to their current state by David Young. That is why our two names are given as translators. But a number of other people have had a hand in the making of *Interferon*. Several of the pieces are substantially or completely as they were when translated and published by Stuart Friebert. I particularly wish to mention "A Special Performance for Statues" and "Teeth," which first appeared in FIELD. Rebekah Bloyd, a student, worked with Holub during his second residency and helped produce preliminary versions in English; her work on "Sundays," "Half a Hedgehog," and "Collision" deserves special mention here.

Finally, I wish to say how much it has meant to me, as the translator with final responsibility for this book, to be able to work with the author, discussing the poems and the choices involved in their rendering in English. I suppose this is a kind of translator's dream; imagine being able to ask Tu Fu, Cavalcanti, Baudelaire or Mandelstam what was meant by a certain line or image! No doubt such an opportunity has its perils as well, but in our case it has all been positive, a partnership and indeed a kind of communion that has meant a great deal and that has, I trust, enhanced the success of the book. If any part of it is mine to dedicate, then I gladly dedicate it to Miroslav Holub, whose presence at Oberlin has been so gratifying and whose remarkable work I feel deeply honored to have been associated with.

Oberlin
June, 1982

BIOLOGICAL POEMS

THE SOUL

In Queen Street
on Friday night
— lights blooming but
already pomegranate-heavy
with Adult Entertainment —
a yellow balloon
was hopping around
among herds of cars,
holding its helium soul together,
two lives left,
to the music of singing ironclads,
hopping, filled with its yellow
balloon-fright
before wheels
and behind wheels,
incapable of salvation
incapable of destruction,
one life left,
half a life left,
with a molecular trace of helium,

using its last resources,
its string searching
for some child's hands
Sunday morning.

BURNING

The fire was creeping along the logs,
whispering curses and weaving spells.
Then it settled into a corner
and began to grow and sing.
It found its speech
in an old letter
from mother.

Orestes' fire. Antigone's fire.
The terrible fire; it's hot
and the black human smoke
rises toward heaven.

SUNDAY

The marathon runners approach the turning
        point:
Sunday, that day of sad songs
near the railway bridge
and clouds.
                Your eyes, at zenith —
and to say this without using the body
is to run without touching the ground.

                Thirty years ago
a transport train went by, open cars
loaded with silhouettes,
heads and shoulders cut from
the black paper of horror,
these people loved someone,
but the train comes back empty
every Sunday, only
a few hairpins and
some bits of charcoal
on the floors of the cars . . .

Who knows how to touch the ground,
who knows how not to touch the ground.

What's left is to believe
in the marathon's finish line
within two hours and forty minutes,
in the deafening roar of clouds
and open, empty cars
on the railroad bridge.

UNITED FLIGHT 412

Megalopolis far behind,
overwhelmed by air. Left over:
a few towers, the rumbling crowds,
the shells on Oceanside Beach
and the gentle yielding of your body
in the atmospheric turbulence
                        called morning.

Thirty thousand feet high
you answered, yes,
I love you, yes.
The Fasten Seat Belts sign came on
and the 727
was set for a smooth landing.

In principle, of course, it was fixed
in the immense white box of sky
like a butterfly
on the pin of a word.

Because where would we be
if love was not stronger than poetry
and poetry stronger than love?

DREAMS

Taking sips from man
like the moon from dewdrops.
The rope grows straight up
from the crown of the head.
The black swan hatches
out of a pebble.
And a flock of angels in the sky
is taking an evening
skid-control course.

I am dreaming, therefore I am dreaming.
I am dreaming
that three times three is nine;
that there is a rule
of the right hand;
that when a circus leaves
the trampled arena
grows green with grass.

Yes, grass.
Grass with no double meaning.
Just grass.

IMMANUEL KANT

The philosophy of white blood cells:
this is self,
this is non-self.
The starry sky of non-self,
perfectly mirrored
deep inside.
Immanuel Kant,
perfectly mirrored
deep inside.

And he knows nothing about it,
he is only afraid of drafts.
And he knows nothing about it,
though this is the critique
of pure reason.

Deep inside.

BIODRAMA

The king of the puppets
is holding a grand hunt
for sausages.
Panicky wursts
and distracted wieners
are scurrying through thickets,
their fat bellies
bristling with arrows.

They are nearing extinction.
The last specimens
are kept
in refrigerated aviaries
of the Babylonian zoo.

The balance of nature
broken again. The bell
tolls for the spineless.

A few foolish children
weep.

AT THE END

At the end of the alley of Christmas trees
and road signs,
at the end of the area where you can pass
the baton in the relay race,
magnetic tapes
and dust behind a carriage,
at the end of the crowd of dummies and dolls,
day-books and night-books,
table and chairs,
beds and eyes,
and cells

a little stumble
on a round pebble

and here it is:
the end of talismania.
But that wasn't the point.

And here it is:
Nobody loves me, everybody hates me,
I think I'll go eat worms.
But that will pass.

And here it is:
the pure literacy of roots,
devoted silence of greenery,
handing over of amino acids, so that
the amber-inspecting technician
won't get angry.
Only from above
the prodigious fugue of fading
genes,
the planetary lullaby,
hardly audible
in all that hush.

So that was the point.
Probably.

DISTANT HOWLING

In Alsace,
on July 6, 1885,
a rabid dog knocked Joseph Meister down
and bit him fourteen times.

Meister was the first patient
saved by Pasteur's
vaccine, in thirteen
gradually increased doses
of weakened virus.

Pasteur died of ictus
ten years later.
Fifty years later
the watchman Meister

committed suicide
when the Germans
occupied Pasteur's institute
including the poor dogs.

Only the virus
never got involved.

THE JEWISH CEMETERY AT OLSANY, KAFKA'S GRAVE, APRIL, SUNNY WEATHER

Lurking under the maple trees
a few forlorn stones
like scattered words.
Loneliness so close
it has to be made of stone.

The old man at the gate,
a Gregor Samsa
who didn't metamorphose,
squinting
in the naked light,
answering every question:

Sorry, I don't know.
I'm not from Prague.

WHEN THE BEES GREW SILENT

An old man
suddenly died
alone in his garden
under an elderberry bush.
He lay there until dark
when the bees
grew silent.

It was a beautiful death, wasn't it,
Doctor, says
the woman in black
who comes to the garden
as always
every Saturday,

and in her bag brings
lunch for two.

THE DEAD

After the third operation, his heart
pierced like an old carnival target,
he woke in his bed and said:
Now I'll be fine,
like a sunflower. And have you ever
seen horses make love?

He died that night.

And another one plodded on for eight
milk-and-water years
like a long-haired water plant
in a sour creek,
as if he stuck his pale face out
on a skewer from behind
the graveyard wall.

Finally the face disappeared.

In both cases the angel of death
stamped his hobnailed boot
on their medulla oblongata.

I know they died the same death.
But I don't believe they're dead
in the same way.

HALF A HEDGEHOG

The rear half was run over,
leaving the head, thorax,
and two front hedgehog legs intact.

A scream, cramping the mouth
open: the scream of mutes,
more horrible than the silence after a flood,
when even black swans
swim belly up.

And even if a hedgehog doctor
could be found in a hollow stump,
under leaves in a stand of oaks,
it would be no help
to a mere half, here on Route E 12.

In the name of logic,
in the name of teachings on pain,
in the name of hedgehog god the father,
the son and the holy ghost amen,
in the name of children's games and unripe berries,

in the name of fast creeks of love,
always different and always bloody,
in the name of roots that grow
over the stillborn baby's head,
in the name of satanic beauty,
in the name of fresh-dressed human skin,
in the name of all halves
and double helices, purines
and pyrimidines

we tried to run over
the hedgehog's head with the front wheel.

This was like operating
a lunar module from a planetary distance,
from a control center seized
by a cataleptic sleep.

And the mission failed. I got out
and found a heavy piece of brick.
Half a hedgehog cried on. And now
the crying became speech

repeated from the ceilings of our graves:

And then comes death
and he will have your eyes.

INTERFERON

Always just one demon in the attic.
Always just one death in the village. And dogs
howl in that direction, while from the other way
the newborn child comes, just one,
to fill the empty space in the big air.

Likewise, cells infected by a virus
send signals out, defenses
are mobilized, and no other virus
gets a chance to settle down
and change the destiny. This phenomenon
is called interference.

And when a poet dies, deep in the night,
a lone black bird wakes up in the thicket
and sings for all it's worth,
while a black rain trickles down
like sperm or something,
the song is bloodstained, the suffocating bird
sings perched on an empty thorax
where the imaginary heart
wakes up to face its forever interfering
futility. And in the morning, the sky's swept clean,

the bird's sleepy, the soil's fertilized,
and the poet is gone.

In Klatovska Street, in Pilsen,
by the railway bridge, there was
a small shop that sold quilts and comforters.
In times when what is needed
is a steel cover for the whole continent,
the quilt business is slack.
The shopkeeper was in trouble.
In such times men of the world
usually turn to art.

In the big shop window
the shopkeeper built
a cottage of quilts and comforters
and staged a performance every night
about a quilted cake-house and a red-quilted
Little Red Riding Hood, while his wife,
in this stuffed masquerade,
played the wolf or the witch,
and he was the padded Hansel,
Gretel, Red Riding Hood or Granny.
To see the two old people
crawling in monstrous floods of textile
around the plump cottage
was not unambiguous.

It was something like the life
of sea cucumbers in the mud
under a cliff. Outside
the surf of war roared and they
carried on their puffy
pantomime, out of time and out of action.

Children used to watch from the street
and then go home. Nothing was sold,
but it was the only pantomime around.

The black bird sang
and the rain poured into the thorax
marked with the Star of David.

But in the actors under the quilts,
l'anima allegra must have woken up
at that moment, so that,
sweating and rapt, they played
the undersea *commedia dell'arte*
thinking there was no backstage
until a scene was over, moving jerkily
from shopwindow to cottage and back,
with the gaiety of polio-stricken Columbines,
while the sound of drums and bugles never
        reached them.

Or else they thought such a deep
humiliation of old age
and its traditional dignity
interfered with the steps
of men in leather coats
and departures of trains
for human slaughterhouses.
It did.

The black bird sang
and the ravaged sclerotic hearts
hopped in their chests,
and then one morning they did not play,
did not raise the shutters,
the sky was swept clean, the soil fertilized,
the comforters confiscated for the eastern front
and the actors transferred to
the backstage of the world
called Bergen-Belsen.
In place of the quilt shop now
a greengrocer peddles rubbery kohlrabies.

Always just one death in the village.
Always just one demon.
How great is the power of the theater, even if
it ends up collapsing
and vanishing backstage.

Dogs howl in that direction.
And the butterfly pursues
those who stole the flowers.

When we did autopsies
at the psychiatric ward in Bohnice,
in air thick with the urban pollution
of relative futility,
the car would pull up before the barracks
and the inmates would wave
some sort of Labor Day parade flags
from the windows
as one went, hugely alone,
to the solitary mortuary
beyond a grove of trees
where the naked bodies
of ancient schizophrenics
waited, along with two live inmates,
one pulling the corpses up from the basement
on a dumbwaiter and putting them gently
on tables, as a mother would
her unbaptized child,
the other lurking in a dark corner
with a pen dipped in ink
to write the Latin protocol,
his spelling faultless,
and nobody uttering a sound, only

the moan of the elevator shaft . . . and the
    knife
slicing the epidermis and dermis made
a sound like tearing silk . . . and it was always
powerful and unprecedented pneumonias
and tumors big as dragon's eggs,
the rain soaked the thorax
and in the roaring silence
one had to break the line of an angel's fall
and dictate the logical sentence
for the ghoul, doomed ages ago . . .
and the schizophrenic's pen in the corner
diligently scratched the paper
like an eager mouse.

We need no prompter,
the puppets said proudly.

The air of this anatomic theater
was filled with interferon,
it was a spectacular personal charge
against the malignant growth, it was
a general amnesty of walls, entropy
was forsworn for the moment,

because there are no bubbles at the bottom
to be cracked by the breeze.

The red balloon outside
soared to the unseen heaven, its chains
stretched by knowing
the nearer the inferno
the greater the paradise,
the nearer the prison cell
the greater the freedom.

Cantabit coram latrone omne vacuus viator.

And that is the fierce essence of the theater,
when the actor stripped of everything
rises to the top of the conflagration
and everything else is hushed
like a much-hunted animal
with muscles still trembling
but with endorphines
and an immense peace in the brain.

Yes, even a whale will sometimes leave the herd
to hurl itself into shallow water and die in the
        sun
like a collapsed cathedral, with a pushed-out
        penis,
and death is buried instantly
in a tiny grain of sand
and the sea is laughing.

Ask felled trees; in broken speech
they preach about saplings. In the galactic
jargon of white dwarves
stars of the main sequence
shine forever.

In the non-Euclidean curved space
which passes comprehension as
the interference of the theater does,
you hear forever the voices of children
from the elementary school of death,
children from kitchen puppet tragedies,
and children from military junkets
when spearing and subsequent flinging of legs
was something like curry,
the condiment of mercenary marches,
voices of children passing comprehension —

But we washed behind our ears,
we didn't pull the cat's tail,
we haven't put
our fingers into sockets —

What else is left
in the universe of hominization
slow as the decay of tritium,
except learning about the growing shame of
        demons —

since the time of the Aztecs, high priests
haven't presented offerings while dressed
in the skin of a freshly skinned prisoner.

We need no prompter, said —

One Christmas, a drunk
dressed up as a devil
fell down the stairs and lay there,
and a child, experiencing
that embarrassing joy just inches from fright,
ran out, upon hearing the noise, and called —

Mummy, come here, there's a dead devil —

And he was, although the actor got up
after another sip. Maybe dogs howled,
but only by a dark mistake.
The stars of the main sequence shone,
the bird was about to sing in the saplings,
the child trembled a little
from the chill of three million years,
in the big air, and was told,
poetically,

it's all just a game,
look, the butterfly's bringing

the flowers back . . . and
there's no other devil . . . and
the nearer the paradise . . .

It believed and it didn't —

TOWARDS A THEORY OF THE THEATER

COLLISION

I could have been dead by now,
he said to himself, ashamed, as if
it was the heart's malediction, lifting a bundle of
    bones
to a man's height, as if it was
a sudden restriction from even touching the
    words —
Danger / High Voltage.
Anyway, he was afraid to find
his own body pressed in that metal. Painful —
down to the capillaries.

The streetcar stood jammed over him
like an icebreaker's bow; what was left
of the car was a funny pretzel
bitten by the dentures of a mad angel.
Something dark was dripping onto the rails,
and a surprisingly pale wind
leafed through the pages of a book
that was still warm.

People formed in a ring and with deaf-mute
sympathy waited for the play's
catharsis, like black mites
creeping from under the wings
of a freshly-beheaded hen.
A distant siren's wail moved closer,
turning solid in the hexed air-conditioning
of that day and that minute.
Dewdrops fell on the back of the neck,
like remnants of atmospheric dignity.
Painful, down to the capillaries.

No thanks, he said, I'll wait;
because a silent film had begun to run,
without subtitles, without colors,
without answers.

And what about magnetic monopoles
fleeing seconds after the Big Bang,
protons violating the principle
of time reversal variance.

The giant molecular cloud complexes
delivering embryonic stars.

The loneliness of the first genes
accumulating amino acids
in shallow primeval puddles,
on the collateral of entropic loan sharks.

Dried starfish
like hawk's talons, grasping the bottoms
of vanishing seas.

Mortal migrations of birds
obeying the sun's inclination
and the roar of sexual hormones.

The caged, half-crazed
orangutan who vomits to pass the time.

Mice that learned to sing
and frogs, balancing on one foot like the thigh
of a Mesopotamian beauty queen.

Poetry, an occupation
so messy it makes the slide-rule bend,
and supervisors increasingly cross-eyed.

What about the girl in the leukemia
ward
on the toilet, wanting to show

what a mustache the good doctor has —
when she gestures with her skinny sticks of hands
she starts to slide through the seat, grabs it,
gestures, grabs, again and again.

And what about the lousy egghead,
the associate professor who almost
understood the approximate universe
and forgot about the traffic rules?

No thanks, he said to some uniform,
I don't need anything. I have my license
in my pocket, but I can't reach it.
And he tried to smile a little
about this painfully embarrassing,
finished creation.
It's all my fault, he said,
thank you.

And then he died.

LANDSCAPES

Yes, you were there, Helen. We were sup-
posed to be picking beets, but the inebriated
veterinarian kept throwing them at us, and we
had to duck as they whistled past our ears. And
he kept asking you to have schnapps with him.
Mud mixed with hate. The photographer fell in
the brook and got badly bruised. An ambulance
was on the way.

But it was peaceful in the distance.
Far in the north, on the ridge,
a fine smoke. Somebody barbecuing somebody.

Far in the west
hunters gathered,
fat as possums. Their jaws

were set to devour the mammals and birds
and pull the whole horizon
out of kilter.

Far in the south —
clouds copulating in grays
and a lightning bolt shaped like a tree
stuck in the earth.

Then the farm officials came and got mad be-
cause the beets were all over the place. Every-
one else was drunk, so they got mad at us.

On the hedge, next to the mousehole,
a butterbur bloomed, confused
by this autumn spectacle,
although it was all
perfectly obvious.

SEEING

A child encounters a mirror and looks.
The child grins and waves.
The child droops the corners of its mouth
and hunches its back.
The child pulls down its eyelids
and sticks out its tongue.

It plays the fool
and the sad sack and
it plays Jack-in-the-box.
Not yet, says the child.
It's not me yet.

Cronus the gravedigger used to get drunk after
funerals and sleep it off in the morgue. Kids
threw old wreaths at him through the broken
windows: Goodbye Forever, Rest in Peace, and
We Shall Remember You. The gravedigger
tried chasing the kids for awhile, then went back

to his digging. At last he crawled into the grave
and looked at the walls. He grinned and pulled
down his eyelids. Not yet, he said. One day he
went instead on his bike to get another bottle,
fell down and broke his cranial bone. He was
lying on the asphalt, his blue eyes wide open and
his face sandy and rigid: he made no faces. Any
more.

Mirrors come in October
and stroll through the city. The images
of images enliven November.

Pedestrians pass each other.
Wait, says mother,
Santa Claus won't find you.

The child is happy, because Santa Claus
prickles. The child mistakes him
for a hedgehog. But it can see him.

Once in the highlands, on a dry, grassy hill, I met
a blind horse at dawn. The horse began to follow
me, taking quiet, regular steps. A huge owl sat
on a bush and turned its head. We went down to
the valley. When we reached the road, I sat on a
stone and waited, wondering what one could do

with a blind horse from the highlands. The horse
stood humbly behind me for a long time. Then it
turned back and walked uphill until it disap-
peared in the skies. The sun was high and a raw-
boned wind began to blow.

We are passing a suffocated pond.
I don't want my gloves, says
the child, and searches with its little hand
resembling a tame finch
for my hand.

I observe
the meeting of hands
in the glassy December light.
I guess it's not me yet.

MEMO FOR A LITTLE DAUGHTER

Behind us, when we don't look back,
the rain and the sky fold up
like a musical score with a part of a trumpet,
the houses and the square are laid aside
in a box lined with newspapers,
the birds become letters
in a secret black folio,
puddles reflecting night and a distant fire
are carried off to the attic
like presents that grandpa gave to grandma.

The streetcars are hidden in cotton-wool clouds.
Pedestrians leave for waiting rooms
and take out their sandwiches
because their walking's over
when nobody's watching:
and a giant spider stalks
on seven long legs through the empty city
whispering lines from the next scene.

It's intermission in the dubious theater
of a thousand actors and one spectator.

When we're away, the home we leave behind
turns into a glassy Bethlehem
under an ancient Christmas tree.
Dogs with eyes like teacups
and dogs with eyes like millstones
carry your princess away from the castle
where philosophers stand on their heads
and the king puts the crown away,
too heavy for a jester.

The flock of other children
flies up to the top of the old elm
and twitters, going to sleep.

When we're away, the home we leave behind
shrinks to a little oval mirror
and our parents act
in the theater of flies
that we know nothing about
because it's a play
beneath the play
and soon night falls.

That's why I used to cry a little

when we had detention at school
and I couldn't go home.

But by now I've got used to it.

Although
I still don't know the play.

THE MAN WHO WANTS TO BE HIMSELF

He throws out the artificial flowers and chases away the electricity. He locks out all voices with a musical key, in two turns. He showers two days and two nights in the dew. He takes an eraser and rubs off all traces of non-self from the self. His skin is as pink as an embryonic membrane now, and his soul is lighter than helium. He floats in his garden, a toadstool cap on his head, fossil leaves on his shoulders. He searches for the little teeth of extinct species and puts them under his tongue.

I am myself now, he whispers to himself in the unknown language of the Aztecs.

He wants to shake his hand, but the hand refuses.

Now the man is looking for himself, but no soap. Not at the bottom, not on the surface, not in the sink or the mirror or under the rug.

No, I'm not worth myself, mutters the man.

I'll have nothing more to do with me.

THE FAMILY IN THE LAWN

In the fall, when there's enough of everything and the bioprogram in the automatic washing machine disappears, they must go out and seek their fortune. The woman, obese as the seventh reincarnation of an Hawaiian guitar, the child like a strawberry groping for words, in the arms of the good man with a red beard and enormously sad shoes, liberated from hygiene.

Nature is as fresh as a sleepwalker's breath.

At the campus of St. Michael's College, the man, woman and child step on the spruce lawn and bury themselves for the winter. Out of sight, out of hearing.

Their apartment is inhabited in the meantime by a raccoon and an opossum, a stork and two mice.

In spring, the lawn grows green, opens, and two heads, four arms and the rest appear, the parents crawl out, go home and ask how things went.

The child stays outside. It sends out roots and is mowed down.

SWANS IN FLIGHT

It is like violence done to the atmosphere; as if Michelangelo reached out of stone. All the swans on the continent take off simultaneously, interconnected by a single circuit. They are circling around, which means that Fortinbras' army is coming, that Hamlet will be saved and the actors will play another act. In all translations, all theaters, behind all curtains, and without mercy.

The actors are already growing wings against fate.

To hold on: that's everything.

A SPECIAL PERFORMANCE FOR STATUES

Solitary statues are introduced into the orchestra, while groups of statues are in the boxes. Someone remembers that bigger statues may not obstruct the sight of the smaller ones. Very small statues are permitted only in the suite of the nonfigurative compositions.

In the first act, there's nothing on the stage. The statues don't like much movement and racket. Vibrations damage their crystalline structures.

In the second act, a black-rock quarry is opened onstage. The rock is torn off the walls and shaped by hammers and chisels. When the shape is born, a pyrotechnist comes along and skillfully places the charges and sets them off. The statues don't like repetitions of their likeness. The statues don't like themselves at all, essentially.

In the third act, a big flock of seagulls is onstage. The birds are spooked by the haze coming from a symphony orchestra down in the trap, and they fly around and into the audience, settling on the statues' heads. There they do the natural things they usually do. The whole scene is irresistible fun. The statues applaud with a minute of silence.

After the performance, the theater is changed into a museum.

Therefore, theaters disappear.

But in the review, Venus of Milo praises the art of using gestures onstage and Nike of Samothrace expresses her satisfaction that the value of the human head is on the rise.

TEACHING ABOUT DISEASES

Puppet diseases are tiny and thread-like, with funereal fur coats and huge ears. And little clawed feet.

There is no fever. Just sawdust sifting from the sleeves.

Diarrhea is like intellectual melancholy.

Irregular heartbeat is like the tick of death-watch beetles.

It doesn't look like a disease, just attentive listening, which falls over the eyes like a hood.

When the strings break, that's the end. Just a carved chunk of wood on the bank of the river Lethe. And at the crossing, the little green man signalling: Walk!

Chin up, shouts the puppet-master. We'll play Macbeth. Everyone kicks the bucket in that play anyway. And the remaining puppets line up obediently backstage and pour out water from their little booties.

THE FUNERAL

When a puppet kicks the bucket, a black spider
weaves a white web around the stage. Two mice
play Sinding's "Rustle of Spring" on the piano.

Then there's absolute silence. The puppet's
     strings are cut.
The puppet is lowered into the piano and the lid
     is shut.
The piano rises and floats in imaginary space.
A long spindly finger emerges from eternity and
     hits the high C.
It sounds for a long time.

A beautiful funeral, thinks the puppet in the
piano, and waits with invalid limbs to get a part
in the shadow-puppet theater.

TEETH

Teeth are a rather ridiculous inside remnant of the outside. Their life is filled with dread that they'll be forced outside again and lost there. A lost tooth doesn't know if it's clenched or revealed in a smile, it doesn't know how to put down roots and so it loses its capacity for aching.

Many teeth have been lost throughout the history of civilization, some by educational and corrective measures in the lives of younger individuals, some by the wasting away of old age. Teeth that have been bashed in during the development of civilizations don't rot, they scurry along in the darkness, scared of daylight. Some just grow tired, and are discovered and described in some new scientific discipline.

Surviving teeth convene on dark cloudy evenings, trembling with horror and telling the old gum stories, fist stories, stories of stiff boots, of other kinds of bashing. These stories are not without some unintentional comic effects, the teeth become comic figures, repeating their plots evening after evening, century after century.

That's how the puppet theater came about.

It's the theater of teeth, for which there's no mouth.

Now close your mouths, children, and listen.

THE MERRY ADVENTURES OF THE PUPPETS

THE CAST

Punch: Pink dress with jingle bells, particularly on the cap. About two feet high, more or less sexless and lacking adrenal glands. Authority on good and evil.

Johnny: Country bumpkin, clear as a forest spring. Member of the local fitness center. Helps old ladies across the street. Collects berries and waste paper.

Princess: Brocade and a tiara of genuine imitation jewelry, made in Hong Kong. Speaks foreign languages as well as the vernacular. No longer pubescent, but still waiting for her dragon.

Dragon: Family Agamidae, with many spare parts, garaged.

Michael the Water Sprite: Four feet high, green and frog-like. Webbed fingers, green hair, red scarf and shoes, water dripping from coat-tails. Freshwater, but often stranded at sea, hence his bronchial catarrh.

Little Red Riding Hood: Red cap on blond hair. Parents have steady jobs, granny is a lush.

Witch: Used to be Red Riding Hood too. Has warts and a big burlap bundle. Easily coalesces into groups of two or four. Fries food in honest-to-goodness fat.

Old Man Skrhola: Rugged type with a simple mind, which allows him his clear-cut views. Dressed in a coat of obscure color and a sheepskin hat, because one shouldn't expose one's head to the wind.

Old Lady Skrhola: Knows her name and address, wears a national costume. Expert on the curricula vitae of the other puppets.

Gruntorad the Magician: Pointed hat and yellow eyes. His cavern is such a mess that minor miracles occur spontaneously.

Doctor Faust: Full beard to cover his neurotic mouth-twitch, which his poodle caught from him.

Matysek the Gendarme: White coat, blue belts from which his drum and drumsticks hang. Huge military hat fitted with a visor. Knows nothing about mufti. Partly makes up regulations as he goes along.

Marguerite: Poor girl.

King: King.

Knights, devils and others.

THE BEGINNINGS OF THE PUPPET THEATER

Originally, in the newborn and toddler times,
Punch, the size of a juvenile lemur,
was prancing in meadows, playing with his
        erector set
and singing dirty songs.
The king ruled the climbing ivy
and the carefree dragon, bastard son of
        infusorians and runes,
was splashing in a drop of water.

The molecular weight of the princess was
about 200,000.

Then the sun rose, and shadows were cast.
Natural selection among the shadows gave rise to
the puppet-master.   The puppet-master
decided it wasn't proper for Punch
to sing dirty songs, for kings to rule the climbing
        ivy,
for cells to make love in a drop of water
and to have the molecular weight
of beautiful women measured.
He decided the proper thing would be
for everyone to have a line and spine.
So Punch, the king, the dragon and the princess
had a piece of wire pushed through the top of
        their heads
and down through the body, quite far.

The massive scramble of primeval procreation
was replaced by the order of dumbness.
Punch became mute, the king cretinous,
the dragon turned to stone, the princess miscarried
and the erector set was scattered through the
        world.

Everything was silent, empty and immobile,
as in a museum of hunting trophies.
It had nothing to do with the theater.
Even folklore was out of the question.

Then the puppet-master fitted the hands and feet
      of the fossils
with threads, so they could be comically jerked,
producing new life. The puppets could grin,
mouths gaping from ear to ear,
accomplished by carving the soft wood,
and recite witticisms copied by classical writers
from other classical writers.

And the ivy grows and grows, from liver to brain,
from cradle to altar, curtain up
curtain down,

accompanied by the efficient applause of children
who don't know about silence
and have forgotten
the uproar of primeval procreation.

PUNCH, THE PRINCESS, JOHNNY AND OTHER CHILDREN OBSERVE THE MERRY GAMES OF KITTENS

A velvety paw but a glaring eye.
Eh bien, n'y touchez pas . . .
The world of games is limitless,
a huge crystal ball
enclosing two
. . . kittens . . .
glitteringly dark,
milkily tender,
prowling roses,
born from a flute,
anxious searchers of warm hands,
scribbling with a claw the smooth side of the
        world,

those two
and a dancing mouse,
whose neck they have snapped,
still twitching its skinny feet.
Tout de même, ils sont comme nous.

JOHNNY

I don't like devils and water sprites.
They don't cast shadows, so they don't exist.

And I don't like things that haven't
passed through the verbal digestive tract.

Sadness comes from the stomach.
Greenness comes from chlorophyll.

When I grow up, I'll show no mercy:
I'll be a dragon.

SIR RUDOLPH, THE KNIGHT

He won the femur fencing match.
He won the belfry-throw, right on target.
He won the 5 x 8 meter race.

He won the quail-devouring event
    and the swan-riding.
He won the Rubicon-jump,
    executing a half-turn.

He won the blood-pouring, from bucket to vat,
    as well as the blood-count.
He won the sackcloth quick-change.
He won the love-song contest
    and was first in testosterone production.
He won the burial
    and then the resurrection.
He won the victory-count.

Then a wooden knot dropped out of his cardiac
        region.
He was glued together with library paste,
    which is the aqua vitae, the elixir,
    of winners.

FAUST

Quite recently
Doctor Faust
was put away in the attic.
His performance was no longer
satisfactory.

He came to think
he really was Doctor Faust.

His poodle passed away.

Wagner the apprentice
delivered the closing speech
and out of each word
jumped a hyena.

MARGUERITE

I beseech you, Our Lady of Sorrows, look down
    at my misery.
I am simply love, I know nothing else. The gates
    of hell
gape just beyond the curtains.
I beseech you, Lady of Sorrows,
will you, during the one hundred and sixty-
    second performance,
make Henry — that's Faust — be careful? Don't
    let him sign with his blood,
let him marry me, let us make love, let the lights
    go out,
let our children live without strings and wires
singing unknown songs that will resound
among the paper treetops.

I know it is only a play.
But only a play has a chance
against damnation.

THE ROSE, NUMBER ELEVEN
(*Wedding Announcement Sample*)

*Props: Little Red Riding Hood with half a granny, in
one piece. A fully upholstered Andromeda
settee. An Orion luxury television set. A prin-
cess and half a kingdom.*

There's no one on the stage.
Silence, like a staring
barn owl. One wall makes love
to another wall. We've killed the fly,
the spider has dried up.

The TV features
mommy and daddy, provisions in a basket,
cottage in the woods, wolf in bed,
woodsman with gun.

But Little Red Riding Hood
leaves the horizontal lines
of the PAL system and crosses
the stage of the sitting-room
to the ramp, sashaying along
to get there in time for her cue,
holding a rose, an embryo
wedding bouquet,

(the TV set is blazing, all the better to see you
with, all the better to hear you),

Little Red Riding Hood stops,
the cue isn't coming,
the rose is slowly wilting,
and everything can be seen too well,
and everything can be heard too well,

the woodsman in the TV shoots,
mommy and daddy are dancing,
because they got half a kingdom
and the upholstered settee,

but Little Red Riding Hood feels sorry
for the wolf; at least he has crossed
his own shadow.

Princess, says the rose with its last gasp,
princess, and that was the cue,
and Little Red Riding Hood is happy
for the moment before the curtain falls
— and the curtain falls fast,
since roses should keep their traps shut.

IN THE BOX

The dragon is licking its wounds.
Devils huddle to keep warm.
The witch gave the princess a shawl
because the poor kid was always cold.
Punch is biting his nails.
Johnny is snoring.
Old Man Skrhola is counting his salary:
it doesn't add up.

From time to time
one of them secretly
crawls out of the wrapping paper,
finds a piece of wire
and looks for somebody's head in the dark.

It's nothing, it's just
to poke an eye out,
in order to have a souvenir
from this season in paradise.

PRINCESSES

To the sound of trumpets,
in tune with jingle bells,
in bedrooms behind closed curtains:
the happy decapitation of princesses.

Their bodies are taken
hostage,
their dreams happen
independently
on the high ceilings
of the shadow theater.

And in the morning, naked in the nakedness
of the other person,
we ask, whose hands are these

and which play was it
that had this immortal scene
from the Dynasty of If.

THE SORCERER'S LAMENT

At first it was too wet.
          So one did not practice magic.
Then the fountains dried up, the yeast
miscarried, water snakes
became watch-chains and
watercolors turned into
the sand of heavenly roads.
          So that it was impossible
          to practice magic.

For a couple of years I was busy
filling out white mouse taxation forms.
The King had a lasting controversy
with the Queen, wallpaper grew ears,
flames rolled up like sheets of linoleum,
and thunder struck the harpsichord.
          So that one could not recognize
          whether one was practicing magic
          or not.

Finally, there was a total shortage
of bats. I made them out of paper,
but they looked more like little flying pigs.
And they were chewed up by thready
        hookworms
of the typewriter strain. The magic wand
got pregnant by a retired saint.
My apprentices took to the bottle.
                In fact, I sort of never started
                practicing magic.

But my great magic is that I'm
still here. With a medium-sized
halo around both heads.

PUNCH'S DREAM

I'll come out before the curtain, trying hard
not to tangle my strings
among the sets.
I'll jingle my bells,
whip off my cap,
and before the puppet-master can collect his wits,
I'll speak in my own voice,
you know,
my own voice,
my own thoughts,
for the first and last time,
because then they'll put me back in the box
and wrap me in tissue paper,
I'll say what I've felt
all through the ages of wood.

I'll say, no matter how silly my tiny voice
sounds, how embarrassingly squeaky,
I'll say the most serious and crucial thing,
I'll speak my piece . . .

I hope they'll hear me.
I hope they'll understand.
I hope they won't laugh.
I hope it grows in the children
and pricks the grownups.
I hope it changes the color of the sets.
I hope it agitates the cardboard
and the spotlight-shadows. I hope it alters
the law of relativity.
I'll say . . . Hello, hello, hello,
And welcome to our show!

HOW WE PLAYED THE GILGAMESH EPIC

Working mainly from the New Assyrian version, our puppet-master wrote a play unprecedented in the annals of puppet theater. Our troupe, he thought to himself, will be easy to cast for this:

Matysek the Gendarme will star as the mighty king Gilgamesh. He knows how to handle the drum and drumsticks, which he'll drop into limbo in Act Twelve. Enkidu, the hairy forest man, will be played by Beelzebub the devil; and the harlot, putting other thoughts into Enkidu's head, by the princess. Old Lady Skrhola will make a gorgeous Goddess Ishtar, she can strip a bit. Utnapishtim, who built the ark in the flood, will be impersonated by Gruntorad the Magician, without his hat of course! And we've got Franz the lackey and Rudolph the knight to take the parts of the gods Shamash and Enlil. But we have a problem with the monsters. The solution: Old Man Skrhola can be Humbaba the Giant, wearing the Dragon's head, and the rest of the Dragon can play the Heavenly Bull, since its leg can be easily unscrewed and hurled at Ishtar by

Enkidu. Punch and Judy can change costumes as necessary to create extra goddesses, snakes, wolves, scorpions and the people of Ur.

In order to make the production okay for children, the puppet-master censored a few of the racy sequences, especially the fornication of Enkidu with the harlot, Gilgamesh's wedding with Ishtar and the edict against cohabitation in the city of Ur. This simplified the play considerably. The rest of the show was to be filled with hurdy-gurdy music, and the harlot would explain the advantages of a school education to Enkidu.

During rehearsals the puppet-master also decided to cut the fights and battles; their educational value was questionable, and the puppets were likely to break their strings. For example, in the fight between Gilgamesh and Enkidu, Beelzebub's nose was damaged, and Doctor Faustus, wearing Lucifer's hairy hide, had to stand in for him. So these scenes were replaced by lectures on geography by Michael the Water Sprite before the curtain.

Then it turned out that the sets
lacked a cedar forest, and that the roaring

of Humbaba the Giant gave the puppet-master
laryngitis. The swords with blades that weighed
two talents each and thirty-pound pommels and
    sheaths
got lost during rehearsals. The elamak-wood
    table,
the bowl of carnelian filled with honey,
and the bowl of lapis lazuli filled with butter
were never supplied.

To have the trap-door open
so that Enkidu's spirit could soar up
from the underworld, like a gust of wind,
was technically too difficult.
But everyone was hamming it up like hell:

Punch and Judy scamper in the square and yell:
    Oaruru, you created Gilgamesh,
    Now create his counterpart,
    Let him face his stormy heart,
    Let them meet and fight, and then
    Let Ur live in peace again.

Hairy Faustus sits in a meadow with the Princess,
    chanting:
    I will challenge him boldly,
    I will cry out in Ur:
    I am the strongest of all,

I am the master of fate!
I am he who was born in the hills,
He who is mightiest.

Then the princess gives her passionate speech:
Eat bread, Enkidu,
It's the staff of life!
And drink some beer, for such
Is the custom of our country!

Matysek the Gendarme waves his halberd and
howls from the ramparts:
I want to help cut down the cedars!
I want to win eternal glory!

Then Michael the Water Sprite lectures on
forestry in Lebanon.
Skrhola enters, wearing the dragon's head:
Let me go free, Gilgamesh,
You'll be master, I'll be servant.
The trees I've grown I'll fell for you,
And houses I shall build for you.

As soon as Skrhola drops dead, discreetly,
his missus under the lime tree cries:
If you don't make the Bull of Heaven for
me,
I'll shatter the gates of the underworld,

105

I'll uproot the gate-posts,
I'll summon the dead to devour the
        living . . .

Faustus promptly throws the dragon's leg at her,
and Franz the lackey plays it very annoyed.

And the puppet-master,
buoyed up by all the action,
keeps telling the puppets what a hit this epic is,
and rushes them round the stage,
jerking their hands and feet at random,
and even recites the connecting texts
in a robust contrabass,
and in the verbal flood
Sumerian remnants paddle around
while the puppet-master bawls:
        Who's the most beautiful hero
        Who's the greatest of men?
and he kicks the spotlight of Shamash the God
while verses are heard through the chaos:
        Along the road of the sun he went.
        One double-hour he traveled;
        Dense is the darkness and there is no light.
        He can see neither before nor behind.
        Four double-hours he traveled;
        Dense is the darkness and there is no light.

He can see neither before nor behind.
Six double-hours he traveled;
Dense is the darkness and there is no light.
He can see neither before nor behind.
Eight double-hours he traveled, crying out:
Dense is the darkness and there is no light.
Nine double-hours, the north wind in his
      face.
He can see neither before nor behind . . .

and nobody knows who is who,
the curtain is torn and so is the cap
of Punch, the friend of children,
and everyone goes home, not knowing where,
and Michael the Water Sprite
before the curtain, still on stage
unharmed by the stampede
quietly quotes Enkidu —

      Heaven was calling, Earth answered.
      And I stood all alone.

and adds, Gee, that's a knockout,
an epic like that.
And anyway, we'll never
get parts like that again.
Never.

ENDGAMES

THE AUTUMN BUS

Exhaling asthmatically, the front door opens. Tripping on the steps, passengers with turned-up collars rush in, burdened with bags and packages. Some hold gloves in their teeth. Others crush morning papers under their arms, feverishly searching themselves for change. Passenger Mrs. Nyklichek carries a child, which keeps sliding down. Passenger Holas waves his fist threateningly at the darkness outside.

The seated passengers, already in transit, watch with hostility.

Driver Chodura turns in disgust from the steering wheel to check the fares as they go into the cashbox. Numerous corrections and additions are required.

Chodura shuts the door, which closes with a screech. The lights are switched off.

The bus starts with a jerk. Passengers fumble around and stagger into its depths. The bus is underway.

Chodura turns to check the last fare.

CHODURA: (*huskily*) From the stunted coppice
        white steam is rising . . .

111

SEATED PASSENGERS: (*in chorus, with relief*)
> For fishermen, abandoned by water,
> For a black mirror with a tenfold
>   image . . .

PASSENGER HOLAS: (*grabbing the overhead bar*)
> For empty veins of roads and ancient
>   paving crews . . .

STANDING PASSENGERS: (*in chorus*)
> For girls guarding dead geese in grass,
> For foreign feathers in the fastidious
>   fire . . .

*Honking. The driver brakes. Passengers not holding bars
lurch forward. Chodura spits through the half-opened
window.*

CHODURA: (*energetically*)
> Snow ripens in the fists of unborn
>   babies . . .

SEATED PASSENGERS: (*getting up to exit*)
> And the spider in the eye sockets begins
>   the story . . .

MRS. NYKLICHEK: (*pushing forward with the child,
excitedly*)
> The tree of ice has sprouted and is
>   broken by the sky . . .

PASSENGER HOLAS: (*at the door*)
>On this earth, we shall never meet again.
STANDING PASSENGERS: (*in chorus*)
>On this earth, we shall never meet again.
CHODURA: (*braking, switching the lights on*)
>On this earth . . .
SITTING PASSENGERS: (*in chorus*)
>. . . we shall never meet again.

The bus has stopped, the door has opened with a hiss. Suddenly, there is a deep, motionless silence.

CHILD OF MRS. NYKLICHEK:
>On this earth, we shall never meet again.

Far away, a honking is heard, but the silence persists. Nobody moves.

THE ANGEL OF DEATH

In an unspecified white hall, maybe the gym of a health resort or just Limbo, a line of corpulent citizens (C1 — Cn) seated on exercise bicycles pedal in pairs in a line from right to left. They wear white t-shirts and baggy, suspicious-looking sweatpants. They do not twitch, look up, turn around or otherwise distract themselves; they just pedal on as if the smooth running of the epoch depended on it.

A good-sized loudspeaker hangs above the row of cyclists, opening its black mouth and speaking in a sonorous, trustworthy voice.

LOUDSPEAKER: Citizens, such is the momentum of life. After the union of sexual cells, explosive reproduction and differentiation occur. The three embryonic layers give rise to tissues and organs and, you see, one begins breathing, digesting, kicking one's feet . . .

The citizens are pedalling more assiduously.

LOUDSPEAKER: . . . humoral factors and mediators are flowing out, thinking has begun, thoughts swim like glass fish in the black, prehistoric sea.

One citizen cleans his ear with his little finger; all keep pedalling.

LOUDSPEAKER: Self is distinguished from non-self. The frontiers of identity and the world are set. . . . The first cells mutate and degenerate, and the clock of life subtracts the first sum from the limited number of cell divisions. Birth takes place. One is leaving . . . for education courses, training, culture. One is exercising and economizing. The unmitigated enthusiasm circulates from capillaries to heart and back again, possibly through the lymphatic system too. One walks cheerfully down sad streets, and vice versa. One gambles in lotteries, and new horizons appear. Love is made. The increased level of sexual hormones ruins the thymus, control of malignant growth declines, malignancies occur, production of IgG antibodies declines, IgM antibodies cross-react with the tissues, rheumatism and diseases of collagen set in, atherosclerotic plates appear in coronary arteries, infarctions knock softly on the walls of the heart chambers . . .

The citizens, one after the other, start pedalling at a frenzied rate, struggling to ride away without leaving the spot.

LOUDSPEAKER: One walks sadly down sad streets, plaster falls. A balcony falls too. Maintenance has always been a problem.

Exhausted, the citizens return to their original speed, eventually wiping off the eventually heavy sweat.

LOUDSPEAKER: Freedom is the recognition of necessity. Here and there the number of cell divisions is exhausted. One is at one's wit's end. Jumping just in time from in front of buses. Buying lottery tickets. Creating values. Working after retirement. Culture is a function of working after retirement. One is turning into one's inward nature. The inward nature is the function of muscular atrophies. Blood circulation is often insufficient. Particularly in some places. Testosterone and a diet are introduced, and teeth are pulled out. It is the time of wisdom and merits.

The citizens pedal on and suffer.

LOUDSPEAKER: And then, citizens, then . . . comes the Angel of Death.

Darkness sets in. A blood-colored glow penetrates from the wings. Ponderous, fatal steps are heard, reminiscent of monotonous kettle drums. From the right enters — the Angel of Death. He is a small scrawny man in a rather shabby dark jacket and striped trousers worn at the knees. Has a forlorn briefcase and a bald head. He stops behind the last pair of cyclists at the right, so that none of the pedalling citizens can see him.

LOUDSPEAKER: An opportunity for you, citizens. A special compliment from the administration. This is your big chance. Speak to the Angel of Death. He stands behind you.

The citizens pedal on silently.

ANGEL OF DEATH: (*suddenly, like a sergeant*) Comrades, atten-shun! Pedal on, citizens, pedal! I'm telling it like it is: exercise, exercise, exercise! Because by exercising . . . You call that pedalling, Olejnik? . . Olejnik, don't sit like a monkey on a melon . . . Because by exercising we strengthen our health. A solid health — hey, Opasek, pull up your

117

pants, they're getting into your chain — a solid health, as well as walks outdoors in any kind of weather — Olejnik, stop staring and pedal — and a strong will prevents diseases. Prevention of diseases prolongs life. We live long — Opasek, put a new drawstring into that pair of pants, you'll never strengthen your health that way. We live long in order to . . . well, Olejnik? In order to . . .

The Angel of Death takes a cigarette out of his breast pocket and lights it. He blows the smoke at citizen Olejnik, pedalling in the pair in front of him.

Citizen Olejnik jumps down from his exercise machine, turns to the Angel of Death, and timidly stretches out his hand.

OLEJNIK: Olejnik, pleased to meet you, sir. . .
ANGEL OF DEATH: Karel Stac is my name.

They shake hands. Citizen Olejnik silently crumples and collapses. The Angel of Death puts his briefcase under his arm and climbs on the empty exercise bicycle.

ANGEL OF DEATH: (*triumphantly*) In order to exercise longer and better . . . We live

longer in order to strengthen our hearts . . .
We live longer in order to longer and better
. . .

*The Angel of Death moans the phrase rhythmically,
and the citizens adjust their rate and pedal in time like
marching soldiers, at attention and fully confident.*

ANGEL OF DEATH: (*pedalling, speaking in a
rhythmic chant*)
    In order to longer and better . . .
    In order to longer and better . . .

CRUCIFIX

At the center of a huge table sits the Judge, in a very worn gown. On either side, the Assessors, made of cardboard. Below the table, right, a bench on which the little bird-like defendant huddles, flanked by beefy warders. Below the table, left, the Prosecutor, standing erect and mostly addressing the audience.

Above the Judge's head is a large crucifix, showing a Christ of athletic build, his loin-cloth rather resembling Bermuda shorts. He puffs at a big cigar, held in his pierced and bleeding hand, now and then tapping ash in front of or on the Judge.

The proceedings are well under way.

PROSECUTOR: . . . of these repulsive crimes, yes crimes, what is especially significant, yes directly and enormously significant, is the pathological, though conscious, yes entirely conscious, even deliberately calculated and calculating affection for animals. Yes, animals.

The Defendant cringes even more.

PROSECUTOR: In his apartment he keeps — as has been testified to by witnesses and proven — he keeps, yes keeps, three cats, twenty-eight mice, five of them white, one iguana, and four, yes four, parakeets. He looks after them, feeds them, day and night. Yes, this . . . this . . . this individual, who has brought such affliction on his friends and neighbors, returns to his lair in order to let white and gray mice out of their cages and feed them on cheese, bacon, yes and bread and salt, in order to stroke, yes stroke with fingers soiled by so many machinations the warty skin of an iguana . . .

The Defendant, visibly shaken and head bowed, covers his face with his hands.

PROSECUTOR: . . . yes, an iguana, so that he could throw it drugged gnats, yes gnats, and give it infra-red ray treatment, so that he could fondle lazy and debauched cats and make them purr, yes purr, while . . .

The Prosecutor suddenly stops as if he has forgotten the text and lost the thread. He crouches apprehensively. At the same moment, the Defendant stands up straight. As if propelled by the same mechanism, Prosecutor and Defendant exchange places with a matter-of-course air of ritual. The Court and Warders do not move. The Defendant now stands in the Prosecutor's place, while the Prosecutor cringes between the Warders.

DEFENDANT: (*picking up the thread naturally, unabashed*) . . . while his fellow-workers and comrades were groaning under the weight of the evil he had wrought. But he, cynically, yes, cynically . . .

The Defendant, drawing himself up to full height and pointing at the Prosecutor crouched between the warders, raises his voice with great feeling.

DEFENDANT: . . . was feeding his parakeets with what the mice had left, feeding them sunflower seed, yes seed, and stale rolls, yes, and even watched those gorged budgies preening themselves and billing and cooing. And this he did at a time when he was causing his neighbors, fellow-workers and comrades so much suffering . . . in the first place, because . . .

JUDGE: (*his concentrated attention distracted, booms out*) Please keep to the point!

The Prosecutor looks up for a moment, but the Defendant thunders on.

DEFENDANT: Yes, to the point. On the very day when so many mice had nothing to eat, when so many cats were whining helpless on the rooftops, when so many parakeets were threatened, yes threatened by polluted air and a shortage of sunflowers, on the very day when some iguanas, yes iguanas, were directly dying out, yes literally dying out, when, for example, only two specimens of the iguana *Ophisalis corneliana* were left alive and one didn't know where the other was . . . !

The Defendant breaks off and looks around in triumph. The Judge gazes idly at the clock.

JUDGE: (*raising his voice, almost hysterically*) Silence in the court! The hearing is adjourned. The Court will consult. Remain in your seats! The hearing will resume at ten o'clock.

The Judge gets up. He is not very tall and his gown trails after him oddly. The Warders also stand, stride in step to the Judge's chair, and grab him by the shoulders. Non-

chalantly, they drag the feebly-wriggling Judge out of the court-room.

Prosecutor and Defendant go up to each other. One offers the other a cigarette. They light up and stand chatting.

Christ throws away his cigar and spits ceremoniously.

PROSECUTOR: You know, his nerves aren't what they used to be. In Disraeli's day, remember, we had trained crickets and eight squirrels —

DEFENDANT: Chickenfeed! Under Vespasian I tossed in a couple of young tigers.

CHRIST: (*uneasily*) Say, you guys, help me down, will you?

PROSECUTOR: What do *you* want? Just hang in there!

SUPPER À LA RUSSELL EDSON

A very ordinary kitchen. Gas stove, shelves. In the middle, a table set for the evening meal, short side next to the wall, chairs placed around. On a chair at the side facing the wall sits the Child. The Mother shuttles from stove to table with a bowl that steams like a fortune-teller's cauldron. Facing the door, a chair with a cushion, on which rests a huge, egg-shaped piece of granite, gneiss or coping-stone. Just as Mother puts the bowl on the table, the door opens abruptly and Father rolls in, wearing a coat and scarf and a stylish little hat pulled well down on his head. As he enters, the lights go up, showing that Father, Mother and Child are wearing masks with a slightly comic grimace.

FATHER: What's going on?

MOTHER: What do you mean, what's going on? Good evening.

FATHER: What's that there?

MOTHER: A stone.

FATHER: Why's it on my chair?

MOTHER: We invited him for supper.

FATHER: Don't give me that. Take him away. He's on my chair.

CHILD: After supper he's going to play with me.

FATHER: Shut up. That's my place and no one else is going to warm his butt on it. It's my place whether I'm here or not. It's my place even if I just spit on it once a year. Take him away. It's my place even if I'm hanging from the bloody ceiling.

MOTHER: Don't shout. We have a guest. You'll spoil his appetite.

FATHER: What am I supposed to do?

MOTHER: If you went for a walk, you'd be a nice sort of passer-by. If you stretched out by the stove, you'd make a nice linoleum pattern. If you crawled into a saucepan, you could be a potato.

CHILD: You could sprout. I'd water you.

FATHER: Shut up! Okay, so you like that hunk of stone better than me?

MOTHER: There's nothing between us. It's just that he looked so on his own we asked him in for supper.

FATHER: I'm also on my own.

CHILD: Go on out, then. P'raps someone's going to find you too.

FATHER: Shut up!

MOTHER: Don't be rude. He'll lose his appetite. I can't stand stones with indigestion.

FATHER: It's my place! It's my food!

MOTHER: When we've finished supper you can take a bit outside with you.

FATHER: Okay, so you mean you've found someone instead of me.

MOTHER: We didn't go looking for anything. Neither did you.

CHILD: I didn't look for anything either.

FATHER: Shut up! You mean to say I forgot to replace myself all these years.

MOTHER: I don't mean to say a thing. I haven't meant anything for ages. I don't know anything.

FATHER: Okay, so now you've got a substitute. I'm going to go and sit down on the street corner and wait. Okay. You don't mean anything. Okay. You don't know anything. Okay. You don't even know whose place this is and who I am?

MOTHER: I'm just putting supper on the table.

Mother lifts the lid of the bowl and clouds of steam fill the room. Father takes off his hat and scarf, sits down at the table facing the stove, and pulls off his mask. He has no face: his head is of the same stone as that facing him.

Mother stiffens over the bowl. The Child jumps up. As if by command, both remove their masks. They too, understandably, have shapeless stones instead of faces.

MOTHER: (*with relief, pushing Father aside*) So take yourself off. I'm just serving supper!

SAND GAME

The corner of a park, lined with fragrant jasmine or mock-orange bushes (Philadelphus coronarius). *In the center a sandpit, all dug up, and behind it a smeared bench of unvarnished wood. Partly hidden by the jasmine, a woodshed, into which we can see through its pried-open door. Inside are shovels, hoes, wheel-barrows, and spilled bags of something or other.*

Seated on the bench is a relatively young white-haired grandpa, wearing a leather jacket and turtleneck sweater. He is reading a newspaper, which he holds open in front of him. Occasionally he peers over it.

In the sand-pit, two relatively big children, Ilona and Robert, are playing. They have built a fairly complicated structure of sand, boards, wire and dog-shit. It reminds one of a rocket launching site or the gardens of Semiramis.

GRANDPA: (*peering over the newspaper*) They say it's going to be very windy and wet. So your fancy tricks'll be blown to kingdom come!
ROBERT: That's not really possible. An anti-cyclone is situated above Norway, but we are

under the influence of very high barometric pressure, which is shifting slowly south.

GRANDPA: (*nettled*) But it's written here!

ILONA: The structure has an adequately firm foundation. We have considered all parameters. This flange here will withstand a pressure of 50 grams per square centimeter. The tolerances are considerable.

GRANDPA: (*more nettled*) You can't make something out of nothing. It doesn't matter a hoot to me what your to...tol...tolerances are. There's going to be a real gulley-washer. That's what they say here.

ROBERT (*adding another little piece of wood*) The information flow is often burdened with considerable background noise. It is appropriate to relate the general and summary estimate to the concrete system which constitutes only a small segment of reality included with the information frame. In point of fact, the micro-climatic conditions of this sandpit can be defined only on the basis of physical evidence regarding all possible features of the regional formation.

ILONA: (*adding a sand patty*) Moreover, the essence of the artifact itself changes reality, or rather micro-reality, to the extent that the information preceding its creation cannot be fully valid, and therefore true, after it has been created.

ROBERT: The case is analogous to every anagenetic influence under natural conditions, which are never identical in relation to the new object nor to themselves, as soon as the object has passed from the sphere of intellectual conception to that of physical realization.

GRANDPA: You're crazy. Yesterday the sunset was blood-red and the birds were flying low. Here they say that a bridge collapsed in Ecuador. Wait a minute . . . not in Ecuador, in . . . what's it called, in Puerto Rico, no, in Malay— . . . in Malaysia . . . no, in Belgium.

ILONA: (*to Robert*) Here a few deep injections are needed.

ROBERT: (*to Ilona*) Certainly. Otherwise this extension would bring about such stress that, with the given material, we would exceed the original parameters.

GRANDPA: (*angrily*) You're crazy. He that mischief hatches, mischief catches. Nothing's going to change that, no matter how much you . . . you parameter yourself!

ROBERT: (*straightening up, though with the patience proper to his age*) In substantial thinking we can certainly relate the value of being, or even the value of its actual statement to a certain pre-formed model, in relation to which the being or statement appears one way or another in-sufficient, inadequate, or excessive. In such a case we can make use of verbal comparisons by means of which we release the dissatisfaction or frustration caused by the imminence of the preconceived model in our thinking, however we may look at it . . .

GRANDPA: Nutty as a fruitcake!

ILONA: But he is furthermore, and in my opin-ion rightly, an adherent of non-substantial ontology . . .

ROBERT: (*beginning to walk about and expound in the manner of the Platonic school*) . . . for only in this way can we rise above the rigid struc-tures of old or new anthropological reduc-tionism and reconstruct our world both in re-gard to its phenomenology and to its freely and operatively substituted existentiality . . .

GRANDPA: (*waving his paper*) Oh, go to . . . Here they say . . .

ROBERT: (*with mounting enthusiasm, which results*

in the appearance of a small flickering and sparkling halo around his head, finally becoming a permanent green glow) . . . to reconstruct the world in its meaningful comprehensiveness, and this, however, in awareness of our being within and consequently from the field we are trying to understand, but also to a certain degree on the basis of abstracting it from our own inness, on the basis of auto-objectivization and ad hoc derealization, which of course is in fact the beginning of real and lasting realization . . .

GRANDPA: You're crazy!

ROBERT: (*his head aglow with enthusiasm, enters the shed, stumbling over various kinds of mess, and is lost from sight*) . . . so that the reconstruction of the world in the system of non-substantial ontology . . .

From the shed comes an explosion, with pieces of flying wood and clouds of dirty black smoke. Ilona sits down on the sand construction, squashing it. Grandpa jumps up, shielding his head with the newspaper. When the noise and smoke subside, a shaken Robert, now without his halo, creeps out of the shed.

GRANDPA: (*triumphantly*) Crazy as a loon!

LENORA

A middle-class room. Heavy, posh furniture, dominated by a secretaire-cupboard, with lots of glass and china, and a row of books. Doors on both sides. In the center, a massive table surrounded by tall, flimsy chairs. An unseen clock ticks loudly. Enter an old man, Libor, and an old woman, Gertrude.

GERTRUDE: What time is it?
LIBOR: (*without hesitation*) Almost eight.

They scurry around like frightened mice, then sprint out, stage left. Enter from the right a girl, Lenora, and uncle Oscar, deep in a serious, evidently conspiratory dialogue. Oscar is arguing feverishly. He's dressed in the bourgeois manner, while Lenora is the one character wearing national folk-costume, with rich ornaments, frills, ribbons and leg-of-mutton sleeves.

OSCAR: (*urgently*) Now when we know where the shoe pinches . . .
LENORA: (*in reply*) Now when we know where the shoe pinches . . .

They sit down at the table, put their heads together. Lenora hesitates and withdraws slightly.

134

OSCAR: (*more urgently — everything's at stake*)
Now when we know where the shoe pinches
. . .

After a long pause, Lenora gives a deep sigh. Relieved, Oscar gets up, lifts a finger warningly, to signify the importance of the impending moment, then rushes out, stage left.

Lenora sits still while the villainous Jan creeps in from the right. He is a hunchback, dressed in tight black clothes. Mischievously, he approaches Lenora. She watches him, surreptitiously and cautiously. Jan sits down and begins to ingratiate himself with Lenora.

JAN: (*sweetly*) Now when we know where the
shoe pinches . . .

Lenora moves away, gets up and gives another deep sigh. She walks to the cupboard, takes out a huge, blue-flowered coffee mug, and sets it in front of Jan. Jan is honored, and cheerfully pulls his chair up to the table. Lenora exits right to fetch the coffee. Jan looks around circumspectly. Lenora returns with a pot of coffee and a sugar bowl. She steps close to Jan and adroitly pours the coffee.

135

LENORA: (*matter-of-factly*) Now when we know where the shoe pinches . . .

With the same adroitness, Lenora kicks the unoccupied chair, which crashes on its side. Jan, in a reflex action, gallantly, bends to pick it up. Instantly, Lenora takes a small folded paper out of her pocket and puts a solid dose of poison into the coffee. She produces a spoon from her other pocket and hands it to Jan.

Jan sits down, stirs the coffee and mumbles.

JAN: Now when we know where the shoe pinches . . .

Jan doesn't like the coffee, smells it and turns to Lenora. She looks away. Jan takes another sip.

Suddenly, a sweet playful song sounds from the left. It is sung by a delightful tenor, with extraordinary charm and intensity. Lenora straightens up and listens. She cannot resist, and cries out merrily.

LENORA: Now when we know where the shoe pinches . . .

Jan jumps up and runs to the cupboard, pulls out a rifle

136

and some ammunition from behind the dishes, and runs to the door, loading. But he begins to wobble.

JAN: (*raucously*) Now when we know where the shoe pinches . . .

Exit Jan. Stamping feet are heard from both wings.

TENOR: (*offstage, exclaiming*) Now when we know where the shoe pinches . . .

A loud shot and a falling body are heard.

LENORA: (*crossing herself*) Now when we know where the shoe pinches . . .

Lenora sits down in front of the table, center. Her body is stiff. All of a sudden, the room becomes very dark.

Libor and Gertrude enter from the right and trudge in front of Lenora without noticing anything.

GERTRUDE: What time is it?
LIBOR: Almost eight.

They trot around and sprint out, stage right.

A number of plain-clothes policemen, attracted by the shot, suddenly rush into the room through both doors. They all look the same, like peas in a pod; all wear mackintoshes and caps. They snoop around, open the cupboard, crawl under the table and dash at Lenora, tearing off her ribbons and frills. They scrutinize them thoroughly and put them into boxes.

Two policemen enter, bringing Libor and Gertrude. From the right, Jan creeps in and flops under the cupboard. Nobody pays any attention.

The police sergeant (mackintosh and cap) switches on a bright light. He turns out to be Oscar. He walks to Lenora and turns on a large floor lamp, turning it to her face. Lenora is stubbornly silent. The policeman shakes her ruthlessly and bangs on the table.

LENORA: (*scared to death*) Now when we know where the shoe pinches . . .

The sergeant writes the words down in a notebook, nodding, quite satisfied.

The policemen are getting ready to leave when the sergeant sees Libor and Gertrude. He gives a signal, two policemen hold them, and he directs the lamp at their faces.

The sergeant stamps his foot.

SERGEANT: What time is it?
LIBOR: I don't know.

DOOR II

Antechamber of an historical event. Heavy brocade curtains. In the middle a massive door leading into there. Above it, a coat of arms, ancient handiwork. In the corner, a solid table and chairs with pompous backs. In front, a pendulum clock, larger than life, ticking relentlessly. It strikes every two minutes, producing a dulcet sound.

Enter Fibbersoldier, investigates the room, listens at the curtain right, at the door, at the curtain left, circumspectly examines the pendulum clock and sets his own pocket pendulum clock accordingly. After which he circumspectly hides behind the pendulum clock.

Enter Captain (beard, pistol) and two soldiers (short swords and notebooks in hand).

CAPTAIN: Come here, Weissberger! Come here, Maximovitch!

Soldiers slouch around, shuffling in various directions, more away from than toward the Captain.

140

CAPTAIN: Well! The decisive moment is near. The greatest caution! caution! is imperative. Everything depends on the three of us! (*Louder*) We have to speak in a low voice. Are we alone?

SOLDIER WEISSBERGER: (*shouts*) We are!

The soldiers stop as far as possible from the Captain. Fibbersoldier lurks and listens. Now and then he writes a note on his cuff.

CAPTAIN: You, Weissberger, get ready at the door!

Weissberger sits comfortably at the table and throws his tools under the chair.

CAPTAIN: You, Maximovitch, will knock!

Maximovitch sits at the table and props his feet up.

CAPTAIN: (*with growing élan, moving down stage*) You will enter and find out if he is asleep!

SOLDIER MAXIMOVITCH: (*behind the table, after a long pause*) He's sleeping like a log.

CAPTAIN: Good! Find out if he's alone!

MAXIMOVITCH: (*behind the table, after a very long pause*) He is.

CAPTAIN: This job is a piece of cake.

He rubs his hands. He sits at the table and takes out a flask, pours himself a gobletful, and drinks it. He offers the flask to the soldiers, who gratefully but lazily take swigs. Fibbersoldier creeps from his hiding place and takes out a goblet, into which he slyly puts a few drops of poison. He hands it to the Captain, who pours. Fibbersoldier hurriedly drinks and hides.

CAPTAIN: Draw!

Soldiers sit. Fibbersoldier lurks.

CAPTAIN: Jump and stab!

Soldiers sit.

CAPTAIN: (*with great enthusiasm*) History is . . . uh what's . . . is watching you!

Soldiers sit.

CAPTAIN: (*excited, pours*) Stab above the fourth rib! As we have taught you! Well! Above the fourth rib, three fingers from the chestbone. Three fingers!

Maximovitch drinks and raises his hand with three fingers up. He scrutinizes his fingers with pleasure.

CAPTAIN: And stab above the third rib too! One never knows!

Soldiers sit and drink. Captain pours diligently.

CAPTAIN: Weissberger, follow Maximovitch!

Soldiers sit.

CAPTAIN: It isn't easy, but you'll make it!

Soldiers sit.

CAPTAIN: (*pours again*) Search the boxes! Take out the papers! Don't step in anything!

Soldiers sit.

CAPTAIN: (*gulps down a gobletful*) Have you got it?

Soldiers sit and stare.

CAPTAIN: (*thrilled*) Have you got it?

WEISSBERGER: (*jerks, after a thoughtful deliberation*) Yep.

CAPTAIN: Splendid! Excellent! The homeland will . . . will . . . always remember you . . . or something. Haven't you stepped in anything?

Soldier W. falls asleep. Soldier M. slumbers, dreamily caressing the leg of the chair with his finger.

CAPTAIN: Cover all the traces! No one must find them. Secrecy and super-secrecy! Stratagems and super-stratagems!

Fibbersoldier crawls from behind the clock, pours himself some poison, taps the Captain's shoulder and hands him the goblet. Captain hurriedly pours.

FIBBERSOLDIER: (*lugubriously*) Thanks.
CAPTAIN: You're welcome.

Fibbersoldier hides again, drinking. Soldiers sit and doze.

CAPTAIN: And now, retreat! Weissberger to the right, Maximovitch to the left! I will send a report to the legate! Hurry! Eye for eye! Death for death! Measure for measure!

144

Everybody sits contentedly.

CAPTAIN: (*with maximum effort and enthusiasm*)
Everything depends on accuracy. Everything
depends on speed. The children will . . .
will . . . learn about it . . . I think! Let us
go! We are flying! We have won! For the leg-
ate! For the homeland! For lawfulness! For
. . . (*he doesn't know, waves his hand*).

*Everybody sits on. The clock strikes. All of a sudden the
door creaks slightly and in the absolute silence begins to
open; it is wide open and gapes. It leads into boundless
darkness.*

*Fibbersoldier, lurking behind the clock, and the Captain
notice it, watch with interest, but do not move. The
soldiers sit and doze.*

*A soft, plaintive sound is suddenly heard from beyond
the door; it gathers momentum, turning into tiny shrieks,
barking, whining, lamenting and culminating in an in-
human, quivering howl.*

QUESTIONING

The greasy spoon Aurora. At the table moribund eaters and drinkers hunch over their plates, beer glasses and cups. At the hot food counter a solitary employee counts bills, which is obviously too much for him. There is an exit from the street, but no other door, because elderliness is not something anybody can pass through. Enter the middle-aged Questioner, dislocated in time and space. He hovers near the hot food counter for awhile, but fails to excite the counting employee's interest. Consequently, he turns to the table of Beer Drinkers.

QUESTIONER: (*timidly*) Excuse me please, can you tell me how to get to the pet store that sells birds?

FIRST BEER DRINKER: (*slightly intoxicated*) Whaddya need birds for, buddy?

In the ensuing silence only the scratching of cutlery in the gravy is heard.

SECOND BEER DRINKER: I knew a guy who had a cricket in a cage. It was some imported cricket.

FIRST BEER DRINKER: Did it make any noise?

SECOND BEER DRINKER: I guess it did. But in fact it was a stiff.

FIRST BEER DRINKER: Well, a cricket won't last, imported or not imported.

SECOND BEER DRINKER: A bird won't last either. I knew a guy . . .

The Questioner tries to attract attention.

SECOND BEER DRINKER: (*quickly*) . . . he used to buy stuff in that store. It's . . . it's round the corner . . . on the way to . . . what's its name . . . to Melnik.

FIRST BEER DRINKER: You crazy or something? It's round the third corner, like you go to the first traffic light and turn uphill, left, you see a sign saying Linen, but they sell surplus vegetables from co-ops, but most of the time the joint is closed.

SECOND BEER DRINKER: Well, you got it all wrong. For sure. It's round the corner, then you go downhill, first uphill, see, and then down, that's the place where old Vokac slipped and fell on Abrham's car and Abrham was just starting the car and he got such a scare he backed the car up and knocked over that vegetable-seller's stand . . . but then he went forward and ran into that old bag's cart, the cart got going and they found it down at the reservoir . . . The vegetable guy ran out and cursed the broad, and she snapped at Abrham, and Abrham was so rattled he forget to step on the brakes and crashed into some garbage cans. Old Vokac was run over by somebody anyway, but no one knew if by Abrham or that cart or that guy who was driving by and stopped to help them . . . Then they all put the blame on that old bag, but she wasn't in her right mind so they didn't get anything from her. So that's where it is, your store, where that cart passed.

The Questioner starts to retreat, but is stopped.

FIRST BEER DRINKER: You couldn't be more wrong, pal. That happened somewhere else, because Vokac went home from the On the Corner pub, and everybody in there heard it and went looking for that cart, because that woman had got lost. What pet store! That store is near the place where that blond broad

used to live, that dame who had five kids and
two daddies for each of them, ten altogether,
so that each kid has a different family name,
but also a different one from the daddies'
names because they could never make up
their mind about it, and she kept forgetting
them. So the kids, they called each other by
their family names, because all the boys were
Peters and both girls were Marys. That blond
dame could never think of any other name
when she got knocked up . . . So the kids
used to hang around at the store window
looking at them birds and monkeys, and
they'd say, see Novak, I'd like that parrot,
and Novak said, no way, Lederer, I want that
monkey, right, Strniskova? So you see, it's
round the third corner on the left, where that
blond piece used to live.

*During the discourse on the blond, eaters at the next
table become interested, and an old woman with a table-
spoon shuffles near from her finished soup.*

SOUP WOMAN: Well, pardon me, I'm sure,
but that blond dame lives at the water reser-
voir, where they had that fire so many times
. . . and she's got eight kids and they (*flour-*

ishing her spoon like a rapier) . . . they once almost burned down that green house, playing firemen, and that green house belonged to old Nemcova, she kept writing letters to her stepson in the army, he'd written her twice that he was killed in action, but he wasn't, he just wanted to get rid of her, but she just kept writing and only stopped when someone told her there was no war . . . so she started fixing up the place, thinking her son was coming back, and she put some old junk in the hall, and the blond dame's kids played there and almost set the house on fire, but the stuff didn't burn too well . . .

The Questioner makes an attempt to withdraw, but the Meat Eater approaching from the next table stops him.

MEAT EATER: (*clutching the Questioner's sleeve, as if intending to drag him to the witness box*) I don't know what you're talking about, but you could see that fire from as far as Vysocany, and it all happened two blocks from here . . . And it was no kids who did it, it was spontaneous combustion. Spontaneous combustion is a special chemical process of unknown origin and I've found out . . .

150

Annoyance and grumbling flare up among the Beer Drinkers.

MEAT EATER: (*with increased effort*) . . . and it is provoked by the contact of two substances, for instance a hard and a soft substance, which makes the soft substance thicken and smolder, while the hard substance. . .

FIRST BEER DRINKER: Stuff it, where do ya get soft stuff in hay?

MEAT EATER: (*ignoring him*) . . . For instance, spontaneous combustion in writings bound in cloth or leather, while in stitched books . . .

SECOND BEER DRINKER: Yeah, but they gotta be rotten inside and you gotta have 'em near a stove.

MEAT EATER: Oh yes, I mean no, my *Health Guide* once caught fire and it spread to *The Classic Legends of Antiquity* . . .

The Beer Drinkers try to stop him and tug at the Questioner's clothes, as if it were all his fault, while the spoon-fencing Soup Woman grabs the floor:

SOUP WOMAN: You see, a fire, it's your destiny. If you are an Aries or a Cancer, and you got white spiders at home . . .

MEAT EATER: . . . and it also occurs when a dull and a smart material get in touch . . .

FIRST BEER DRINKER: Yeah, Abrham once went from the Bistro . . .

SOUP WOMAN: . . . and white spiders make white webs, and if they get into somebody's home, the person will die of fever or fire from those white webs . . .

MEAT EATER: . . . for instance, one Sunday afternoon, Stendahl . . .

FIRST BEER DRINKER: . . . and Vokac got run over for the second time . . .

SOUP WOMAN: . . . They don't see them white spiders and think they got black ones, but the fire is already on the roof. . .

SECOND BEER DRINKER: They got a fine mess at home!

MEAT EATER: . . . and therefore, he keeps his slim volumes of poetry . . .

They all flock together, shouting and waving their arms. The Questioner disappears in the sudden commotion.

SOUP WOMAN: (*shrieks*) . . . and those who

have white webs in their hair . . .

FIRST BEER DRINKER: And Vokac got up and he says to the kid, Novak, where's that monkey . . .

SOUP WOMAN: . . . and whoever kills a white spider is sure to drown, like that old Nemcova, when she fixed up her place . . .

MEAT EATER: Because poetry also begins when dull and smart matters touch, tough and soft . . .

SECOND BEER DRINKER: And Vokac wrote on the wall: There's no Abrham // Abrham is gone!

SOUP WOMAN: . . . People don't know they have webs and no hair . . . But the webs keep catching and catching . . .

FIRST BEER DRINKER: Abrham said he couldn't run him over . . .

SOUP WOMAN: And the spiders were waiting and waiting . . .

Suddenly they all fall silent, because a skylark flies up above the counting employee, flutters below the ceiling, followed by their eyes, and sings as if a ploughman walked happily through his field. A cricket can be heard between the skylark's trilling notes. From the back emerges a king-size bird dressed in a hat and overcoat, and walks hesitantly among the tables.

FIRST BEER DRINKER: (*matter-of-factly*) Get a load of this! Must be some loony in that crazy outfit. What were we talking about?

FAIRY TALES

A room in a cottage, cozy and warm. Real sweet home. In the corner, an old-fashioned stove. On the walls hang ancestral portraits, saints and statesmen, shelves with particularly big tins with spices, among which bay leaves look most prominent. There is no table. The stove faces a large window, strangely bare. Right under it is a stool with Granny on it, and other stools around with a finite number of children. Only the lamp at the stove is lit. It is almost dark, and the clear window seems to let in a strong night light.

GRANNY: (*with traditional kindness*) Once upon a time. In a green castle above the black forest lived a king and he had three daughters. But he was not a good king. He spoiled the ship for a ha'porth of tar, and there wasn't enough food to lure a mouse from a hole. The king was lantern-jawed, hatchet-faced and spindle-shanked. The princesses were always poorly. They had no servants and had to make two bites of a cherry left from breakfast last for lunch. Things went from bad to worse and they literally lived on air . . .

While Granny is speaking, a man in a leather coat and beret slowly emerges behind her back and presses his face against the window. The gleaming eyes stare inside, grow brighter, glow and glare. Hands with fingers spread touch the glass. When the figure has covered the whole window it suddenly disappears, probably stabbed or shot.

GRANNY: (*slightly halting*) . . . that they literally lived on air, so the king called his three daughters together and said . . .

An enormous rooster's head turns up behind the window, opening its beak. A clawed paw pushes forward and tears it down. Feathers swirl as if a flock of ravens has landed.

GRANNY: . . . and he said: Dear daughters, I don't know what to do! I'll soon be pushing up daisies, and if this goes on, you won't get married till the cows come home. You have to wander in the world a bit. First . . .

Feathers swirl and a beautiful naked girl or something similar appears. She clutches at the window, but a bull's head rises behind her and black hairy hands seize her breasts and pull her down. A distant sound of broken glass is heard, long echoing in gusts of wind.

GRANNY: (*speaking louder*) First you, Annie. Take that dress out of the wardrobe, so you don't look like Job's turkey . . .

In a chaotic confusion, heads of cyclopes rush to the window, heads full of teeth, heads full of snakes, sticks full of eyes, trees full of legs, hands, hooves and stumps, and they soundlessly try to break in.

GRANNY: . . . go through the black forest . . .

Shadows of ghosts spill in, flutter through the room and cover everything.

GRANNY: . . . when you come to the village, knock at the door of the first cottage.

Like a shot, everything disappears, but the window and the wall split in the middle and frosty white light flows in. From the distance, two men in coats and berets approach with terrifying ease, spreading a black, growing cape. The cape covers more and more space with an impermeable black shade.

GRANNY: . . . when Johnny opens the door, tell him . . .

The music grows louder and fills the space. Then, in double-quick time, everything is as before. The window with the strong light, walls, the room, cozy and warm, portraits, tins with spices. Children on stools. But there is no Granny. Only the empty white stool. However, as before Granny's voice goes on:

VOICE FROM THE EMPTY STOOL: Once upon a time. In a green castle above the black forest lived a king and he had three daughters. But he was not a good king. He spoiled the ship for a ha'porth of tar, and there wasn't enough food to lure a mouse from a hole. The king was lantern-jawed, hatchet-faced and spindle-shanked.

One of the children, who have so far been quiet and immobile, turns to another.

CHILD: (*with a cheerful gesture*) I dig it, don't you?